All rights reserved. No part of this book/publication may be reproduced, stored in a retrieval system, or transmitted in any form or by any means, electronic, mechanical, photocopying, recording, or otherwise; without written consent from both the author, and publisher of Exposed Books Publishing, LLC, except for brief quotes used in reviews. For information regarding special discounts or bulk purchases, please contact Exposed Books Publishing at info@exposedbooks.com.

© 2020, by Leslie Crawford of Exposed Books Publishing, LLC

All rights reserved, including the right of reproduction in whole or in part of any form.

ISBN 978-1-7348081-5-5

Library of Congress Catalog Card Number 2020908291

Mya Teaches Confidence Through the Alphabet

www.theliteracyshop.com

Written by: Leslie Crawford

Cover Design: Skylar Ogunshakin

Printed in the United States of America

Mya Teaches Confidence Through the Alphabet

By

Leslie Crawford

This book is dedicated to every child out there that has the desire to be whatever they choose to be. For every boy and girl, be confident in your career choice. You are more than capable of being anything you set your mind to.

Thank you to my son Markeice that has stuck with me throughout this journey.

From the time Mya could understand, her parents always taught her about being confident. They told her she could do anything and be anything she wanted to be. Now at the age of 10, it was Mya's turn to teach her 2-year-old brother Markeice the same thing.

Markeice, we had career day in school yesterday, and I saw so many different careers from my classmates. I'm going to teach you about the different things you can be when you grow up. As long as you're confident, you can do it.

A a

Have you ever thought about going into space as an **ASTRONAUT**?

You could fly around in space like Mae C. Jemison. You might meet an alien if you're lucky.

B b

What about a Bus Driver?

You could take everyone to school or work on your bus. Your job would be very important because you have to get people to their destination on time.

Cc

Maybe you could be a Chef. You don't eat a lot of food right now, but when you get older, you can make my favorite dishes. I wonder if you'll be able to cook like the famous B. Smith.

D d

I know what you could be, how about a Doctor?

You can help heal sick kids or even adults. I know you would make a great doctor because you already have a good heart.

E e

Sometimes I think about being an Entrepreneur. I wouldn't mind being my own boss and being able to offer jobs to other people.

F f

What about a Firefighter?

They help save lives by putting out fires. I even saw one rescue a cat from a tree.

G g

Markeice, you could ride around in a big truck collecting trash. As a **Garbage Collector,** they help keep our city clean. We should always want to keep our streets clean.

H h

I hope when you get older, you'll love sports. If you do, I think being the **Head Coach** of a team is a great idea. My favorite team is the Baltimore Ravens, would you like to coach in the NFL?

I i

When I get some money, and you're older, I will buy you some crayons. You can learn how to draw and become an **Illustrator**. I hope you'll be able to illustrate a book one day.

J j

Mr. Williams at my school is our Janitor; he keeps our school clean. This is a very important job because keeping the school clean helps avoid kids getting sick. Mr. Williams makes sure the school stays clean.

K k

Do you remember the blanket Aunt Jane made for you? She's a Knitter and love making things for other people.

L l

A Lawyer is a great career because you get to help other people. Mommy and daddy always expect us to help others. Did you know our former first lady Michelle Obama is a lawyer?

M m

Uncle Marvin owns a body shop. He works on cars every day; maybe you could be a Mechanic and fix cars for a living.

N n

A Nurse is someone that loves and cares for their patients. You have to go to college, but it's a great career.

O o

You could be an Optometrist and help people see better. I have to visit my Optometrist once a year to have my eyes checked.

P p

I don't know if you have noticed, but there is a leaky faucet in the bathroom. If you were a Plumber, you could fix it for us.

Q q

I don't know too much about a Quality Control Technician, but my classmate Jennifer told us that her mom is one. She told us they check to make sure the things we buy are safe for us. Safety is everything.

R r

I think you would make a wonderful Radiologist. They help diagnose and treat injuries and diseases.

S s

My friend Maria came as a School Crossing Guard. They keep us safe when we're crossing the street for school.

T t

I dressed as a Teacher because I want to make the world a better place.

U u

Daddy watches baseball a lot; you should think about being an Umpire. You will get to see the games for free.

V v

There is one career you could have that will help millions of people. You could be the Vice President of the United States.

W w

What if you were a Writer?

You could write a book and be famous like Toni Morrison.

X x

An X-ray Technician works with the radiologists in reading X-rays. You'll get to see the patient bones; I think that's cool.

Y y

Our neighbor Mrs. Carla is a Youth Counselor. She works with children every day.

Z z

I love animals, and I hope you do too. Do you think you would like to be a Zoologist? You can take care of the lions, tigers, bears, and more.

Markeice, I hope you learned something today. I don't know what I want to be when I get older; I think I still want to be a teacher. Whatever I decide, I know I am capable of being anything. I can be a teacher, lawyer, bus driver, or a mechanic. You can be anything you want to be as long as you're confident. Confidence is key.